Preface

Offer all and everything; afterwards, give more. These monologues were written for the sole purpose of guaranteeing, an actor's development, wow factor, and success in all auditions. Each monologue beyond these pages is given great care to accomplish this mission. Furthermore, the monologues have vague abstracts; purpose, expand the actor's technique of constructing concrete backstories and stronger personalization. Only stage directions are established to guide you through the 1 to 2 minute monologues. Furthermore, to mimic actual dialogue; fragments and run-on sentences are utilized intentionally. In addition, both sexes are able to showcase their talent, without compromising their sex/gender credibility with each monologue. Dive in and contemplate every word and punctuation. Gather the confidence and trust within yourself, to harness these monologues. The blueprint has been displayed, solely you, can build the skyscraper to stand on. Break a Leg!

To God, Arlyene

Contents

Good-Bye of Last

You:

I thought you left, years ago. What, your joke isn't over yet? Your joke. Come on! We all know. It's the one where you fooled me into losing my virginity. You got what you wanted; yet you come back? (Pause) (Laugh) So that's it! (Suddenly Serious) You got what you wanted, but you left what you needed. (Pause) (Softly) My love. (Pause) I ran after you for days, walked for weeks, crawled for months, and I'm just exhausted. You left with my identity, but untainted my soul, so I'll stand up again! (Near tears) I'll lie for days, rest for weeks, and FLY for months. (Overwhelming emotion) I'll journey to find a new identity, venturing further then space itself. (Air of Confidence) But first you must go. Don't come back. Don't look back. For this is the good-bye of last.

Big Break

You:

(Tone of Defiance) Don't ask me when, how, or what. For it is driven by a why. Since, the utterance of actor left my tongue; I was compelled to search its verb. Why? Because I was different, the stage permitted and loved my existence. Different, you hear, not similar to unique. Uniqueness is an envied trait praised by society. You understand? I am DIFFERENT. According to western civilization different equals problem. Problem equals outcast. Myself naïve, to fragile, failing to recognize my potential as a (with disgust) societal disgrace. At last! I've gathered a confidence so pure and rich my body trembles from the power. (Pause) I'm going somewhere to let it *ooze* thru every pore of my body. Be there when I do!

Social Networks

You:

I really don't get it? It is really fucking pathetic. Social

networks! It's the most absurd method of (mime quotes)

"connecting" with somebody. Especially, "connecting" with

the opposite sexes. These social networks are outright

outrageous. You can't smell, touch, or hear the person.

Sight, sure, if you're pushing it. To help with these

limitations, we created acronyms such as LOL. I'm scared.

I've witnessed persons use LOL, yet have the most un-

Laughing Out Loud faces. The worst is during *actual*

conversation, they will replace the joy of *actual* laughter,

with LOL! It's the epitome of annoying. (Slight pause)

You know, I too was brainwashed into social networks. I

mean that shit was awesome. It gave my esteem new

heights. I had a system! Steal the most liked post on my

news feed -- Ooh my favorite though, uploading baby

pictures and pictures with my mom! Classic. (Pause)

However, one day I logged on to view my all-time high, 12

notifications. One from Farmville, one from Mobsters, and

TEN fucking LOL comments from mother!

White Flag

You:

(Nonchalantly Surprised) Whoa way to run into you. You still look amazing, wow. (Interrupts) Don't try to say the same for me. Truly, appreciate the attempt at kindness though (Chuckles). (Pause) How've you been? Fantastic? (Seductively) Yes, you are. (Attempts to repair damage) Wait a sec; I haven't seen you since college. I'm dazed that's all. I'm sorry. (Grateful) Thanks. (with a hint of arrogance) Besides, stop flattering yourself. I'm joking! I kid, remember. (Takes a moment) I miss you. Meet me halfway here; I'm waving a white flag. I wasn't allowed to forget you. Your eyes, your hair, your laugh. Yeah, that laugh. I refused to settle, for I had already surrendered my love, to the best. Let me have you, only to miss you again when I say goodnight. Let's begin with dinner.

Coco Milk

You:

Curious? You don't have to answer right away. Feel free to take your time on this one. Help me rationalize, why you are drinking chocolate milk when your lactose and tolerate. Ssshh! Take your time on this. (Physically repulsed) Oh my gosh, you already started. We are in the library, the library. You can't hide anywhere or blend in, they're never crowded. I understand your uh, signature is silent, but it smells so loud! (catches another waft) You do this on purpose, don't you? It's not funny. (another waft) Ahhh, someone save me from this chemical warfare. (Suddenly gets very angry) Take another sip from that cup, and I'll call 911 for attempted manslaughter from the arse! (Long Pause) What is that? Looks like a sandwich. Looks like my sandwich with extra cheese. A bite in it? You didn't! (flatulence answers question) Ahh you did! Cops are on their way

asshole, no fucking pun intended.

Vraiment

You:

(Slow and Controlled) It was a choice. You made the choice, I do. Afterwards, the choosing of whom to love ended. Exactly identical to yesterday, done. The choices you made yesterday are complete. It is impossible to go back and alter it. You can't switch the shoes you wore, amount of money made, or how many times you fucked, yesterday is past. But tomorrow everything and anything can be altercated except forever us! (Pause) At that altar, where you breezed that gold band thru my fingers, mine, smooth thru yours. We became past and future, yesterday and tomorrow. Nevertheless, you chose to shit on that beautiful wonder. Now I have to as well. I only pray, it will permit me to decide of what is left *today,* for tomorrow comes soon.

I vs. Me

You:

(With extreme humble vanity) Looking in the mirror, I see *I* not me. I pride myself far above it all. Scold me, for being arrogant, pompous, and even contemptuous. But the opposite is far worst. Insecurity, stupidity, a pushover, no, I'm quite content with the developed I. The I's are the beings that conquer this world. Evident, by Julius Caesar, *I* came, *I* saw, *I* conquered. The Me's are fortunate to survive it. Consequently, never again find the audacity to tell I, there is no spot for me. Curse you for trying to destroy this foundation of self-worth by trying to hurt. Ignore the politics accept the evidence. Rejecting my talent, are you ashamed? No matter. It's okay. I forgive you. I will continue to fight and slay every giant in my way. Even if I end up having to say instead, I came, I saw, I TRIED. Asking once more, is there a spot for I.

Money Trees

You:

(Condensing smoothly) What is it that you want? I'm rich. You can have it. I'm a walking money tree. Hhmm, all I ask is that refrain from requesting my heart. My heart is fragile glass shattered. Fearful if it falls again, no amount of glue will mend it once more. Forgive me, if I have dramatized to you. Ahhh, my brain is off limits as well. I've taken great strides to procure and polish philosophes or lifestyle procedures, if you will. I rather they not be compromised by another. (Pause) Uh, well that is peculiar! That only leaves my body to question. Permission granted. (Reacts to repulsion) Honey, hold on. In this case, it is what it looks like. An über-sensitive, intelligent, excuse the reference (hesitates) to sexy for their shirt individu-- HONESTY! I'm trying it for the first time, don't make it my last. (Pause) Cool. By the way, I'm not rich.

Unsealed

You:

(Overwhelming emotion) From me *to* you; I could just cry.

My soul has reached the brim. Find the courage to say those

words before I completely tip over. (Painful compassion)

The antidotes for this poison, an unrequited love, are those

words. (Pause) I get it. Life's compass pointed you a

separate way, where new choices and romances were made.

Nonetheless, release me. Please! So, I may too journey a

direction towards new choices and romances; as those words

my needle and satisfaction the map. (Points finger) You

withheld your disclaim; I naïve, to feel shame. Unburden

me. The past isn't far away, its right here. (Very Slow)

Sincerely, authentically, genuinely; let it be. Truth is not a

monster. It is a gift, to me *from* you.

Quiet Time

You:

The bathroom, the most relieving setting of my day.

Whether I like it or not, I'm mediating ten to fifteen minutes

per day. It's unnaturally calming. Nobel Peace prize? Toilet

is winner. Zero disturbance. People so kind to always run

out of your way. Always wonder if I'm in the South! It's a

messy business but babe it gives you the clearest conscience.

Yes, I'm alluding to number two. Number two alluding to

shitting. My advice, pace yourself, maximize the output of

this purity. You're not on a rollercoaster people. The t.p.

isn't you admission ticket! (Mime) It's an ancient scroll

only displaying it hidden message, till the end. (End Mime)

What! Don't fake, you don't look at yours too? You bigots!

Fine. Whatever. I happen to identify time as the greatest

escape artist in history. Subsequently, to balance that art, I

have my own art. I metamorphosized my number twos into a

downward breathing technique, that literally empty's the

soul. Now if you'll excuse me, I'm late for my

Mens'/Womens' appointment.

On the Low

You:

Hey. (Pause) I kinda of miss you. I guess it's to be

expected. I-I I don't know. I let you go. I severed every

form of communication. I was done, and I'm still am. I

blatantly told you to fuck off. It was cool though because I

was the one chasing you. I was the one that was "creep'n."

So it was chill. But you didn't let me go. You didn't sever

any communications. (Pause). YOU weren't done. I was

dumbfounded, it appeared as if you wanted me to stay, hold

on to me. I guess that why I kinda of miss you, instead of

just missing you. You relished the idea and practice of me

chasing you. You blindly continued charming yourself. You

refused to acknowledge the reality within our fantasy. You

believed it to be a race, when it was a game of tag. And if

you intend of playing tag with no tag- backs, most politely,

go fuck yourself.

Toast

You:

I'm so comfortable. I want to sleep right here, right now.

Better yet fall into a mini-coma. That would be my

superpower, the ability to fall into and out of comas

whenever I pleased. The moment I felt like life's bull was

heading toward me, I'll just slumber. Once it passes over,

I'll just wake up. The experience would hold the

equivalence of a time machine. Dream for a month there, a

year over there, maybe a decade! (Pause) People would

miss me right? I'm not a menace to society, but I'm not

exactly a contributor either. (Chuckles) Sounds like the

definition of a moderate. (Pause) I smell something. That

scent, it's familiar like a memory, de-ja-vu. Raindrops are

hitting my face, but clouds are absent. Why do I feel soft

lips are upon mine?

Boss

You:

I like you, but I don't like you. I want you, but I don't want you. I could love you, but I don't know what love means. I'm not indecisive, I just don't understand. Why do I have to accept or reject any of the above? I'm pressured by an unknown source, to pick heads or tails; when both or neither are options too. There is nothing impractical or immoral about leaving those questions suspended. I'm a two-way street, heading east and west. Still, we will not move unless the imperative is met. So I'm asking you to be my Valentine, not because I adore you or anything of the sort. It's because I can. Coincidence.

Wednesday

You:

I have no idea what I'm doing. I'm not the only one. Seven billion people are on the same team as me, what to do with my life. Seven billion people versus am I leaving my mark on this world. The matter of the fact, we are all just competing for time. Whatever it is we claim we are doing, we strive to complete before time. When you ask me what I'm doing with my life. I don't know! I just pray there is enough time to do it. For a life with no regrets is a happy one, complete. When I hear that last tick-tock, when I punch out for my shift, when Coach calls me the bench, I won't care. I won't care about the pay day missed, or my sub-in at the tiebreaker. Because seven billion people will find satisfaction in whatever I do.

Stripes

You:

Don't make it a nightmare. You see (hmph) I have to crush on you. And it has to occur on first sight. It's not a developed thing, rather instantaneous. I am sorry my mistake, I lead *myself* on. I wanted so bad to want you, but honestly I *never* liked you. It's safe with never because someone else won that prize. (Pause) I was pressured by friends, even my family to further mature by means of a committed relationship. (Pause) It was me, has become a figure of speech; still know it was not you. I fucked around with you for eight months; I was listening to everyone expect myself. In the end, it was nothing more than a wonderful distraction. So, thank you.

Dirt

You:

If you want to do something, here's an idea. Do it. If you can't make it at least impulsive, stop trying your want. You're stealing my time. You say what you want to do, yet you're still taking to me about it. The conversation should contain a positive relationship of present or past tense verbs relative to the future ones. (Slight pause) Why is it the desire to change life-styles, habits, or wellbeing, only given serious action when death loses it attraction? Even if you lived 100 years would it be enough? Or instead would you *urge*, to pour over the next century with one more. (Pause) Do it. Only the dead can afford procrastination.

Lifeguard

You:

(Slowly) I am always drowning myself. (Pause) It could be pathetic. (Pause) I don't know why these memories flood me so, only occurring when I'm alone. It just happens; foolishly hoping it's happening to you too. Grabbing for you attention, I know the whistle is mute. Then realizing I'm blind to not notice the sun is in your eyes. (Pause) Even as the water pukes my lungs, and the flashes begin, you save me still. The absence of air is here; nevertheless the rhythm of my chest keeps beat, still. It could be pathetic, I have no care. I'll evaporate soon.

Swinging

You:

(Dreamy) Looked up. (Pause) I caught you staring at me today. And you know, if it was a second before, you would've caught me. But it was too late. Stealthily, we fell into romance, quietly my heart danced loudly. (Scuffs) One could weigh the world on this continuous tension. Unfortunately, for everyone, I'm selfish. Fortunately, I'm reckless. I'll collapse the tension with I like you since I love you is too light. So I'll plummet and shatter; would you perhaps do me the favor of putting me back together.

No, Yes, & Yes

You:

(String the No's and Yes's with beginning and end of sentences) You want to hear a joke. No. You want some giggles and chuckles. Yes. Well, that pisses me off! No. I do not detest laughter. I'm not Dick Scrooge. (Pause) I have a certain perspective. (Pause) Life isn't a comedy. It's a completely different genre, bitchedy. Yes. Life is a bitchedy. You foolish people are too ignorant to laugh *with* it rather than *at* it. Backhand life a few times and dare tell me you are not happier. Yes. No. Shit will still happen, but it won't really touch you.   You're on the outside, laughing *at* it. Get it, yes. YES.

Collide

You:

I'm about to let go. (Pause) Whenever someone walks in a room; my jaw rotates to the direction of the *mystery*. It is complexingly tortuous. It takes all the physical and mental energy stored in my soul to fight the prophecy. Afterwards, I'm too exhausted, to resist the appearance of the next person; I fall into the temptation, solving the riddle. (Pause) I found out early, the reason for this behavior. It's due to the insane notion; if I don't look, *you* will pass me by, failing to begin the chase. It's crazy because I don't know you yet. I eerily desire to fall into the pits of phenomenon to pure myth, love at first sight. It's a curse, the sensitivity to beauty I possess; the gift, the ability that I have to attain it. Hence, the suffering, for once the beauty is won, a new step is placed on the ladder. And I have longed than reached the top.